For Owen who lives
on planet Earth.

IF FOUND PLEASE
RETURN TO NASA

HELLO SPACE

IS ANYBODY OUT THERE?

David Mackintosh

Published by the
Natural History Museum, London

Waterhouse –
the Museum Mouse –
lives here.

At the Natural History Museum.
Cromwell Road, South Kensington,
SW7 5BD, London. United Kingdom.
The northern hemisphere.
The world. Planet Earth.
The Solar System.
The Universe.
(*To be precise*).

Alone inside the Museum at night, Waterhouse has time to think.

Sometimes he thinks about outside.

Out there, *way out there*: *in the Universe*.

Thoughts like:

Do OTHER mice...

...live in OTHER museums...

...on OTHER planets in the Universe?

Waterhouse wonders:

If millions
of animals and
plants of all
shapes and
sizes can live
on Earth,
then couldn't
other planets
be the same?

And if
they are,
HOW CAN
WE
KNOW?

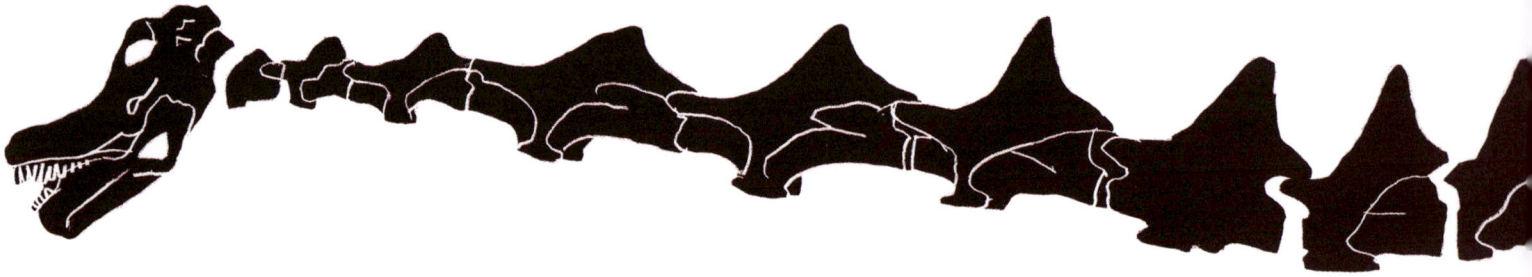

Living at the Museum, Waterhouse has learnt that four ingredients are needed for life to exist.

If these are present, there is a good chance there is life. Or *has been* life:

1. WATER

Everything that lives has water in it. An adult human is 60% water (and a mouse is 80%). *Water is everywhere.* Water covers most of the surface of planet Earth. It has even been found on Mars.

EXIT

Gift
Shop

WATER
H$_2$O
WASSER
AGUA
ACQUA
EAU
VAND
PAANI
MAA

There's
plenty of
water at the
Museum.

2. ENERGY

The Sun is the closest
star to Earth. It gives light
and heat – or solar energy –
and this makes it possible
for life to exist on Earth.

For a star
93 million miles
from here,
it sure
feels hot.

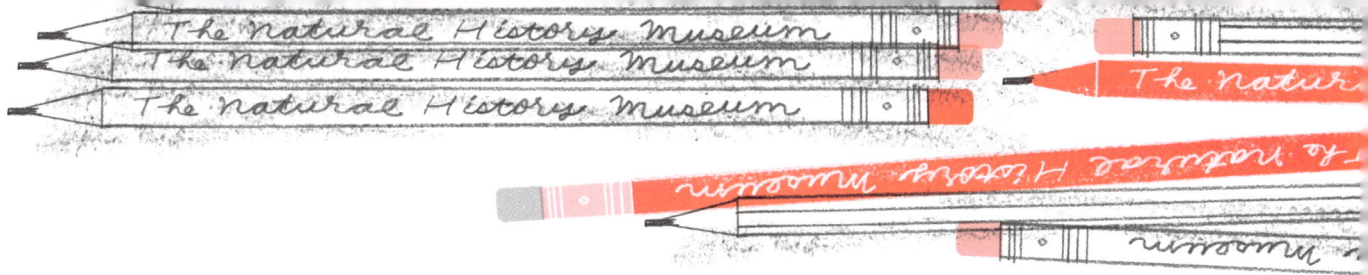

3. CARBON

All living things have carbon in them.
The human body is about 20% carbon.
The lead in your pencil is carbon,
and diamonds are carbon too.

4. JUST ABOUT RIGHT

When the temperature of
a place is just about right
for life to exist, the place is
called *the Goldilocks Zone*.
Mercury is too hot for life
and Jupiter is too cold,
but Earth is just right.

LOOK! Earth **definitely** has all four of those things.

"But how do we know for sure if other planets are like Earth when they are all

SO FAR AWAY!?"

This is CERTAINLY a

Outer space
IS far away.
We need to get closer.

One way is to travel there from Earth.

We can send astronauts in big rockets to other planets. They can land, take photographs and collect rock samples which scientists can study.

However, it takes lots of fuel for a rocket to leave Earth, let alone travel through space to a planet millions of miles away.

IT ALSO SOUNDS DANGEROUS. Isn't there a simpler way to see what's happening way out there?

Powerful telescopes on Earth can see objects billions of light years away.

There's one in Chile, South America, called the VLT: **The Very Large Telescope**. But even big telescopes can't tell scientists everything they want to know.

Space telescopes,

like Hubble and James Webb, are sent on rockets deep into space to get a better look.

little EASIER on the eye.

I can't believe they actually call it The Very Large Telescope.

NASA made the first moon landing in 1969. This was the first time humans stepped onto the surface of the moon. The astronauts collected samples of rocks and soil, which scientists are still studying today.

It would be easier if pieces of asteroids and planets would just come to us on planet Earth.

ASTEROIDS

moons. own their have some and craters, have odd-shaped, are They and tumbling rotating

are large rocks that orbit the sun,

There are **millions and millions** of pieces of rock travelling through space. Some are huge, and some are smaller than a grain of sand.

When it reaches the surface of the Earth...

...it is called a METEORITE.

IF FOUND PLEASE RETURN TO NASA

ARCTIC CIRCLE

Only about

75,000 meteorites

have been found on Earth.

There are many more just laying
about waiting to be discovered.

OUCH! There's ONE NOW!

When meteorites are discovered they are sent to scientists all over the world.

The scientists examine them with microscopes...

some of the meteorites are made of metal, some of rock, and some are a mix of both.

But HOW ON EARTH can they tell where they came from?!

This meteorite was found in Mexico and contains a lot of carbon - one of the 4 essential ingredients. Scientists use the tiny white specks on the meteorite to work out the age of our Solar System.
****

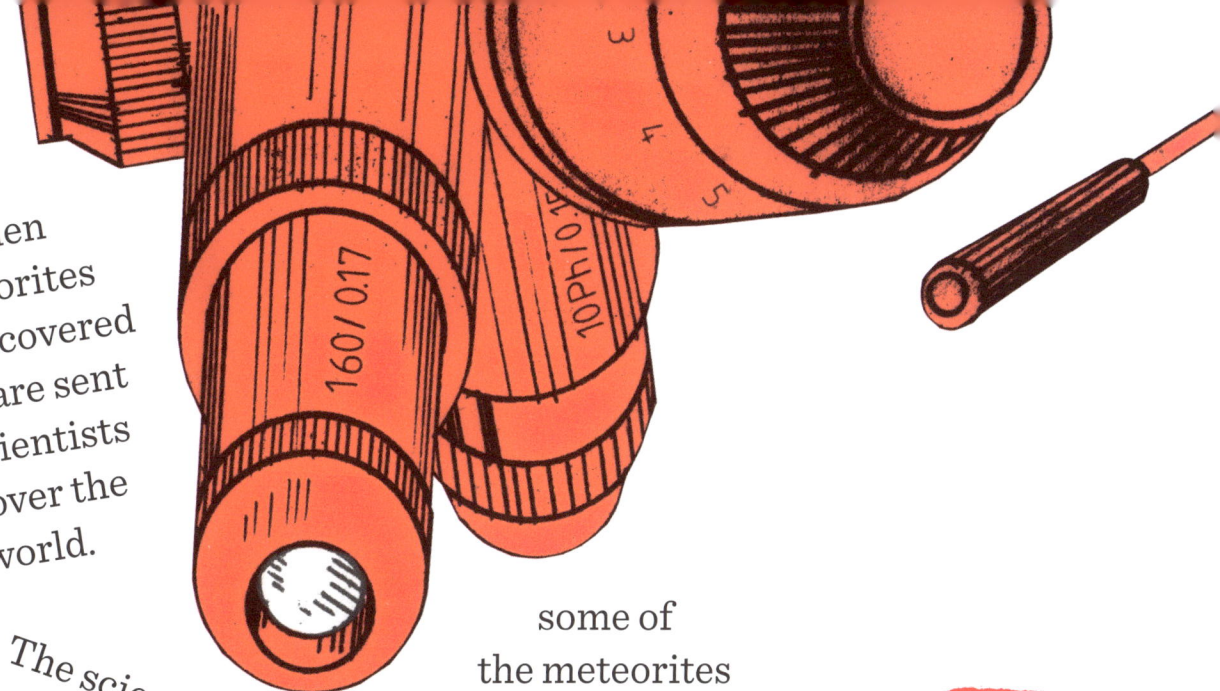

PROPERTY OF THE NATURAL HISTORY MUSEUM (LONDON) (UK) (THE WORLD) (THE UNIVERSE)

ALLENDE CV CHONDRITE BM.1988,M24

1 2 3 4 5 6

Scientists can see
if the meteorite
contains water.

If it does,
then they
know

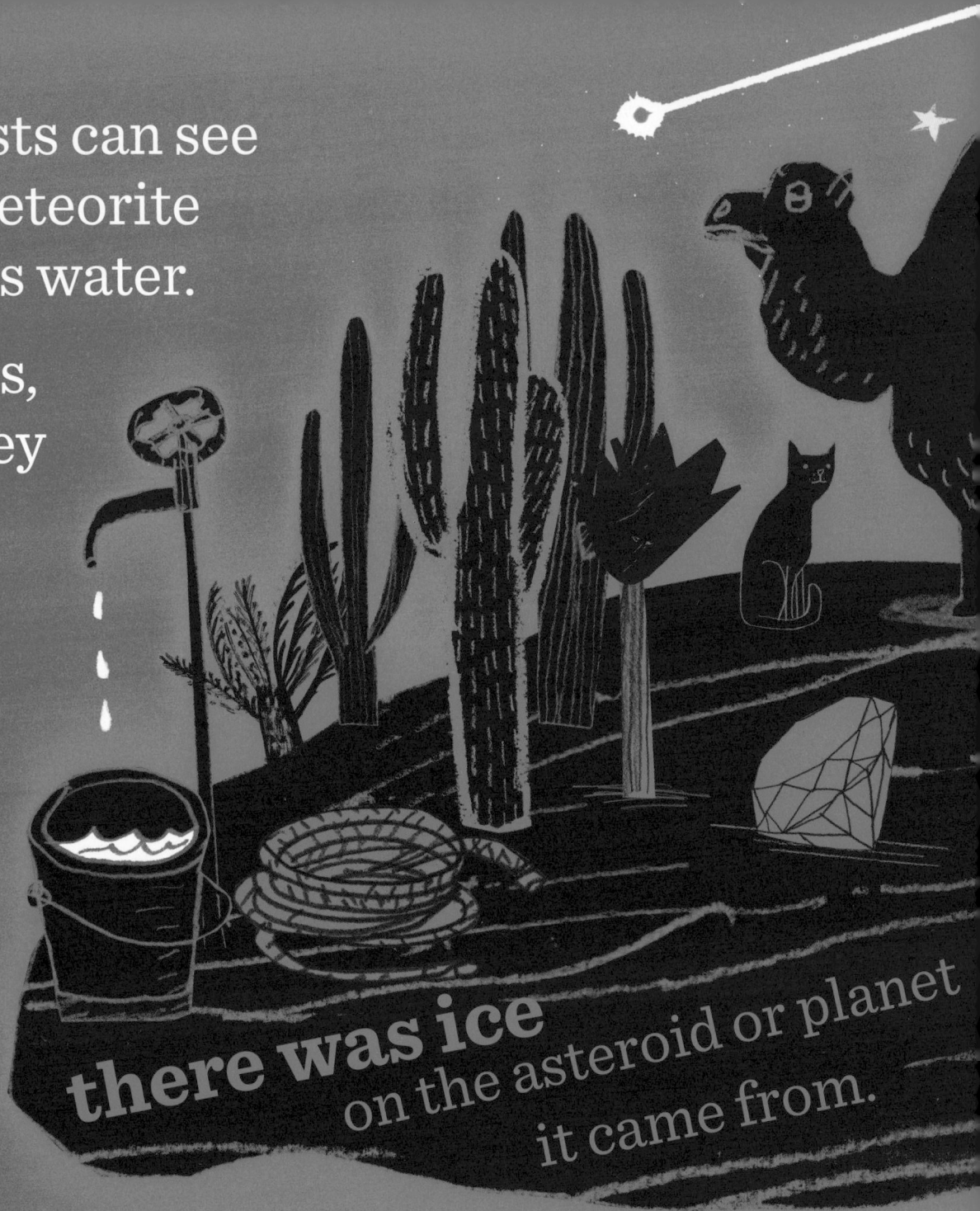

there was ice on the asteroid or planet it came from.

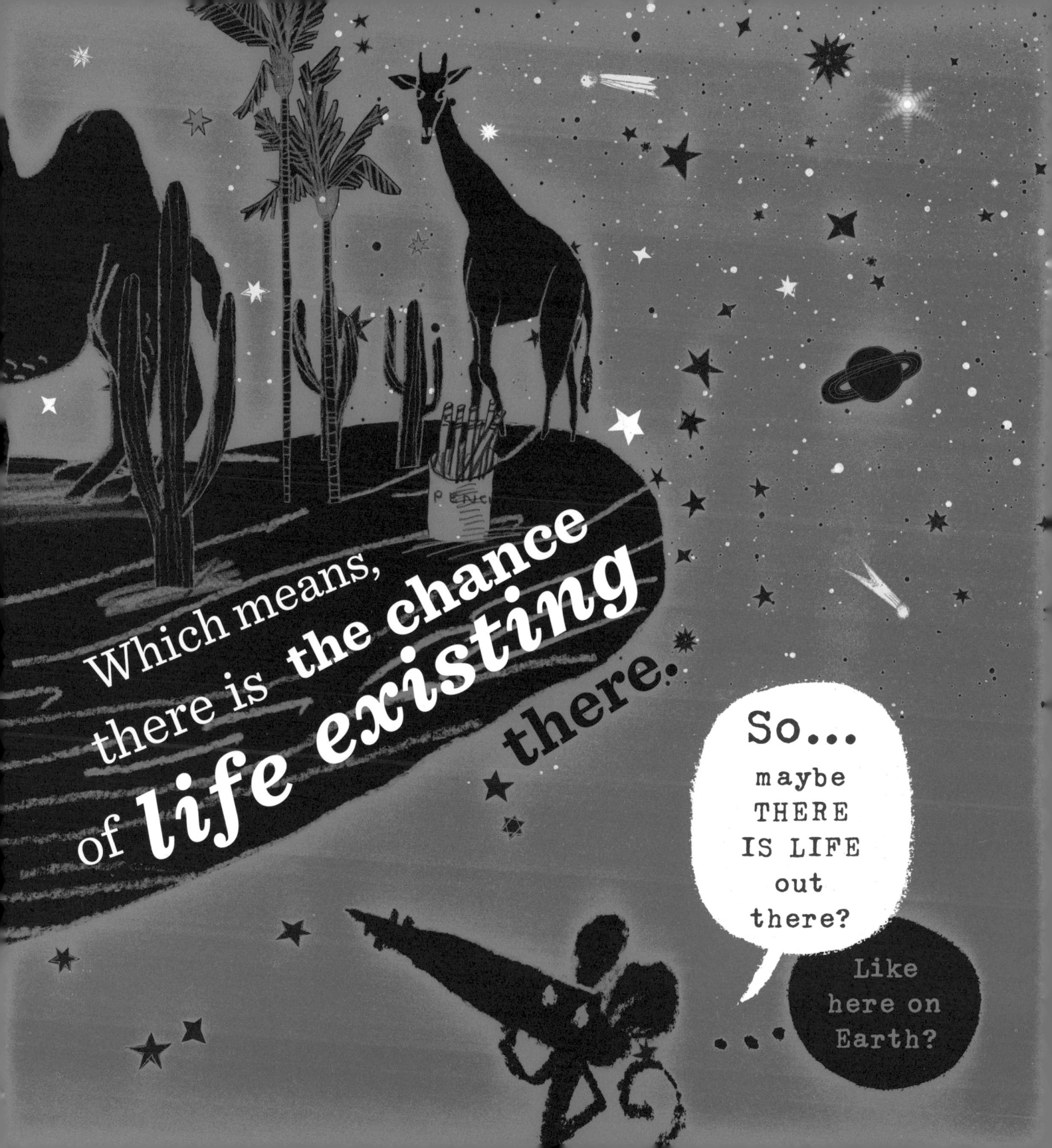

Which means, there is **the chance** of **life existing** there.

So... maybe THERE IS LIFE out there?

Like here on Earth?

We know life exists in the most extreme environments on Earth.

From freezing polar landscapes...

...to the darkest depths of the **deepest** ocean.

Humans have learned to exist in extremes too – *including outer space.* But it hasn't been easy.

The deepest humans have gone is 10,927 metres into the Challenger Deep. The crew included astronaut Kathy Sullivan who was also the first American woman to walk in space.

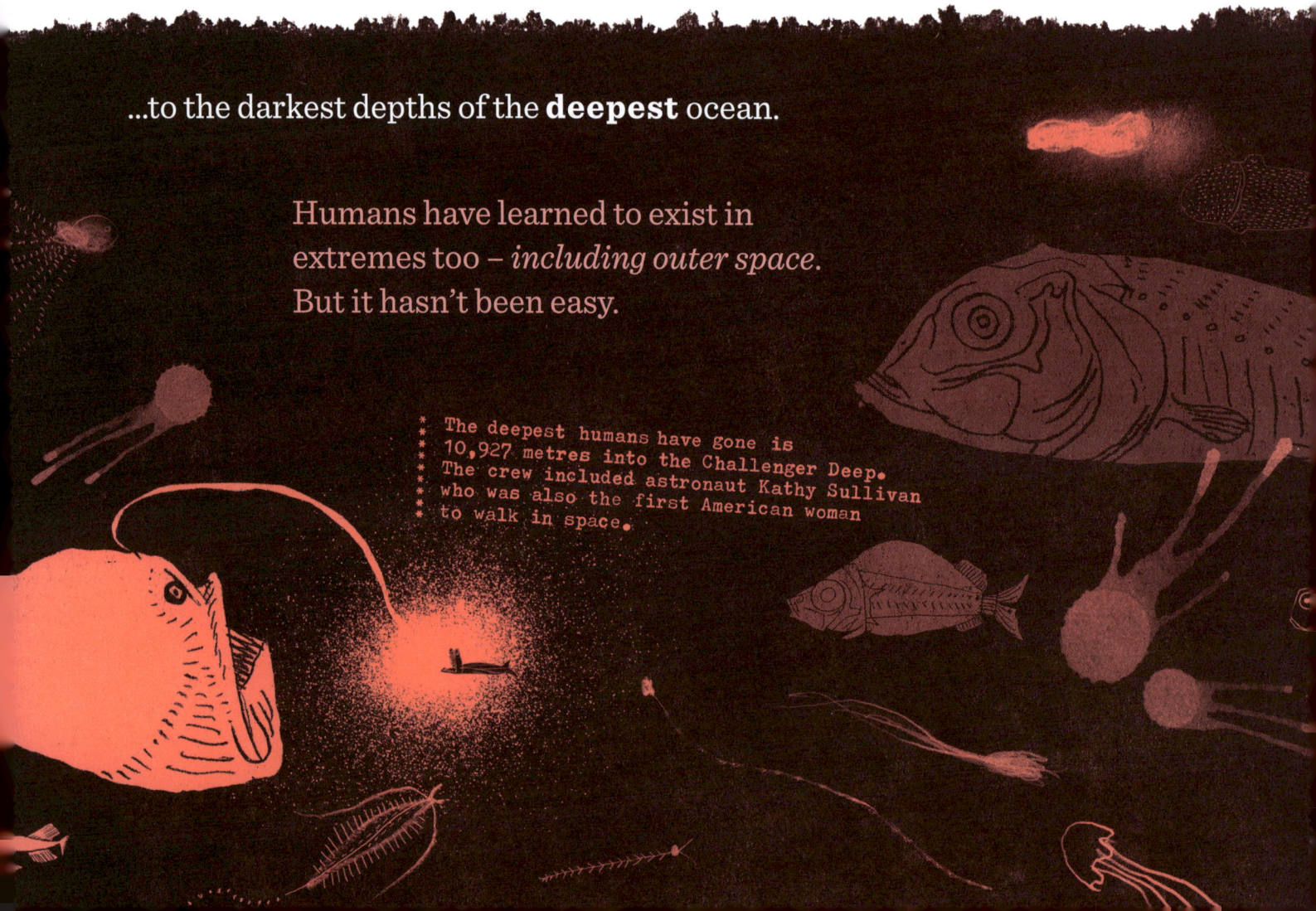

BRITISH ANTARC -TIC SURVEY

"But what about life on OTHER planets?...

can't we just GO THERE AND FIND OUT?"

Scientists already use robots to explore the far reaches of outer space.

Robots can travel across the surface of other planets. *They can even land on speeding asteroids!* They drill into rocks, take samples and send any information they collect back to Earth.

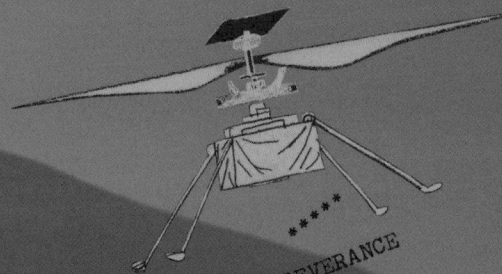

The rover PERSEVERANCE is now collecting samples on Mars. PERSEVERANCE is the size of a car and carries cameras, solar panels and other scientific instruments.

PERSEVERANCE carried a small helicopter named INGENUITY, which was the first aircraft to fly on another planet.

It's difficult and dangerous work, but we learn lots about whether there is life beyond Earth.

In time, humans may be living on other planets, and learning even more about what's there.

Back here on Earth, we can learn a lot from life, too.

Scientists collect specimens of living things to help us understand life better and how it exists in different environments.

The Museum has **millions** of specimens that have been collected over **centuries**.

MAY CONTAIN NUTS.

Wax Model by G. EDWARDS c.1926.

I wondered what all those jars were.

meteorite. 192

Voy. Challeng

187

Earth took **billions** of years to evolve into what it is today.

So for other planets, it may just be a matter of time.

I wish evolution would hurry up.

IF SWALLOWED SEEK MEDICAL ADVICE

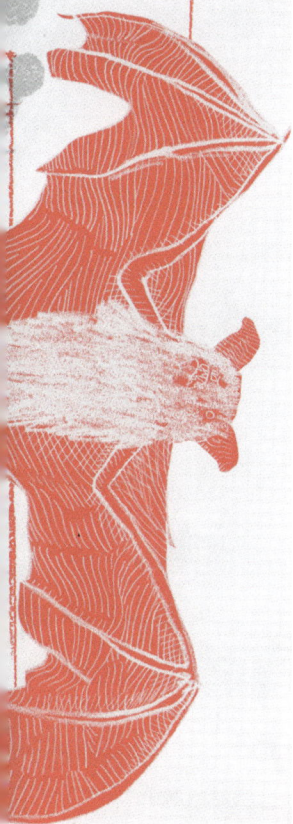

Animalia
Anthropoda
Insecta.
Dolichoderinae
Iridomyrex.
purpureus.
Hymenoptera.
Formicidae

CAUTION: OBJECTS IN MIRROR ARE FURTHER AWAY THAN THEY APPEAR

In the meantime,
Waterhouse will have to be patient,
like the rest of us.

First published by the Natural History Museum,
Cromwell Road, London SW7 5BD.

© The Trustees of the Natural History Museum, London, 2025.

A catalogue record for this book is available from
the British Library.

ISBN 978 0 585 09578 9

10 9 8 7 6 5 4 3 2 1

Text & illustrations by David Mackintosh
Designed by David Mackintosh
© David Mackintosh 2025.
www.profuselyillustrated.com

p. 21 Allende meteorite,
© The Trustees of the Natural History Museum,
London

Reproduction by Saxon Digital Services

Printed by Toppan Leefung Printing Limited

With special thanks to
Dr Natasha Almeida and Prof. Sara Russell
at the Natural History Museum.

THE NATURAL-HISTORY MUSEUM